E.P.L.

I WANT TO KNOW ABOUT
Amphibians

by Dee Phillips

NEW
FOREST
PRESS

I WANT TO KNOW ABOUT
Amphibians

Publisher: Tim Cook   Editor: Valerie J. Weber   Designer: Matt Harding

ISBN 978 1 84898 525 4
Library of Congrees Control Number: 2011924961

U.S. publication © 2011 New Forest Press
Published in arrangement with Black Rabbit Books

PO Box 784, Mankato, MN 56002

www.newforestpress.com
Printed in the USA
15 14 13 12 11 1 2 3 4 5

Picture Credits:
(t=top, b=bottom, c=center, l=left, r=right)
Alamy: 22c. OSF: 19. Shutterstock: Front cover, 1, 2, 3 (all), 5 (all), 6b, 8b, 10 (all), 12 (all), 14b, 15, 16 (all), 17, 18 (all), 20b, 22b, 24b, 26 (all), 28 (all), back cover. Science Photo Library: 6c, 7, 8c, 9. ticktock Media Archive: 4, 11, 13, 14c, 20c, 21, 23, 24c, 25, 27, 29.

CONTENTS

AMPHIBIANS

Words that appear in **bold** are defined in the glossary.

A World of Amphibians

Amphibians live almost everywhere in the world, except Antarctica, very dry deserts, and some islands. Adult amphibians lay eggs, which **hatch** into **larvae**. The larvae live in water. As they grow up, their bodies change into their adult form. They can then leave the water to live on land and breathe air.

Some amphibians live on many different **continents**. Others live in lots of places on just one continent. Some amphibians live in only one country, such as Australia or Japan. When you read about an animal, see if you can find the place where it lives on the map below. You can also look for the part of the world where you live.

This world map shows the continents in bold uppercase letters and countries in bold lowercase letters.

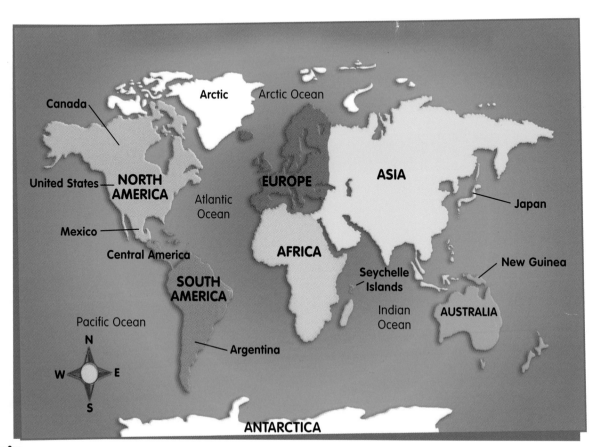

Where Do Amphibians Live?

Some animals live in hot places, such as deserts. Others live in forests or in the ocean. The different types of places where animals live are called habitats.

Look for these pictures. They will show you what kind of habitat each animal lives in.

grasslands: dry places covered with grass

lakes, ponds, rivers, or streams

mountains: high, rocky places

rain forests: warm forests with lots of rain

temperate forests: cool forests with trees that lose their leaves in winter

underground: the dirt and rock under the earth's surface

What Do Amphibians Eat?

Some amphibians eat only meat, fish, bugs, or spiders. Others eat only plants. Many amphibians eat both other animals and plants. Look for these pictures to tell you what kind of food each animal eats.

bugs or spiders

fish

meat

plants

snails and shellfish

Axolotl

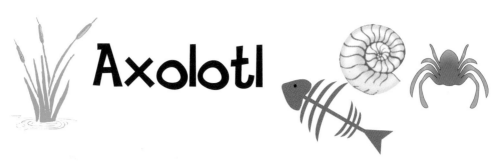

Most amphibians spend their early lives underwater. Then they grow up and live on land. But axolotls (AK-suh-lah-tuls) spend their entire lives underwater. They rarely take an adult form.

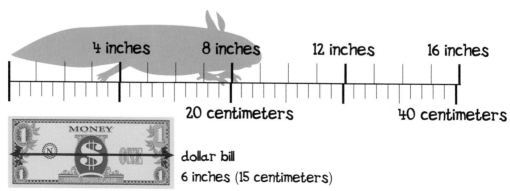

4 inches   8 inches   12 inches   16 inches

20 centimeters   40 centimeters

dollar bill
6 inches (15 centimeters)

In the wild, axolotls swim in a few lakes in Mexico. **Scientists** study these amazing animals. If an axolotl loses one leg, it can grow a new one!

A strong tail pushes the axolotl through the water

Its **gills** look like feathers.

A long fin runs down its back.

An axolotl does not have eyelids. It uses its tiny eyes to find **prey**. It eats worms, insects, and small fish.

Caecilian

Alhough a caecilian (sih-SIL-yun) looks like a worm, it is an amphibian. It lives in Africa, Asia, and the Seychelle Isands, and from Mexico south to Argentina.

Caecilians range in size from 4 inches (10 centimeters) to 60 inches (152 centimeters). Their skin can be many different colors.

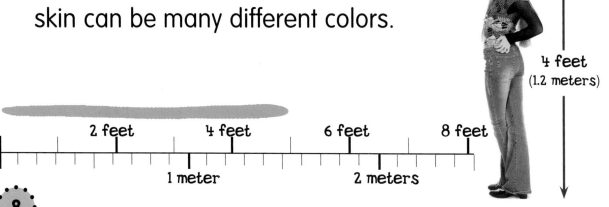

4 feet
(1.2 meters)

2 feet   4 feet   6 feet   8 feet

1 meter   2 meters

Caecilians tunnel underground to find termites, caterpillars, and small worms to eat. They are nearly blind and hunt by sense of smell.

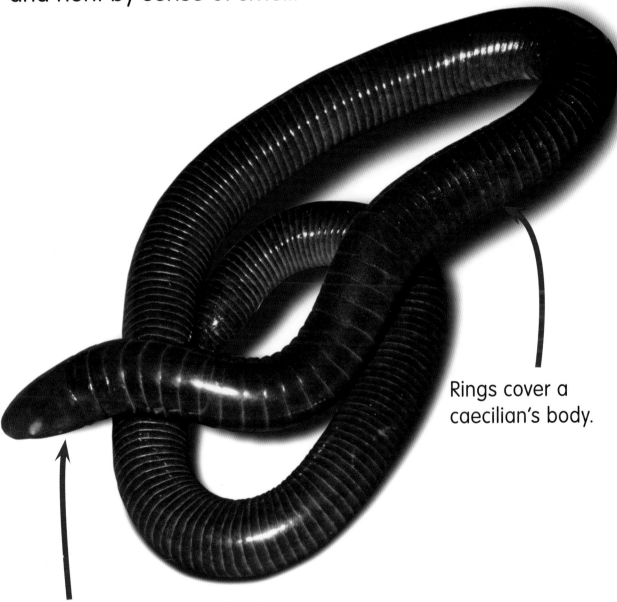

Rings cover a caecilian's body.

Its strong, rounded head helps it dig through the dirt. Curved teeth help it grab its prey.

European Common Frog

European common frogs are the most widespread frogs in northern Europe. They live close to lakes, ponds, rivers, and streams. They spend most of their lives on land and return to the water to **breed**.

Female frogs lay thousands of eggs at once. The eggs look like a big clump of jelly.

If the weather is warm, baby frogs will hatch from the eggs in two weeks. Baby frogs are called **tadpoles**.

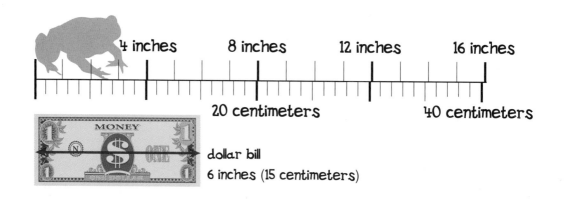

4 inches   8 inches   12 inches   16 inches

20 centimeters   40 centimeters

dollar bill
6 inches (15 centimeters)

Frogs catch bugs with their long, sticky tongues. They also eat snails, slugs, and worms.

European common frogs can live in cold climates. Some even live close to the Arctic!

European Common Toad

The European common toad lives across Europe. It also lives in parts of Asia and Africa.

European common toads spend the day in cool, damp places. They come out mainly at night, looking for bugs and **slugs** to eat.

Female toads lay long strings of eggs in ponds. Tadpoles hatch from the eggs.

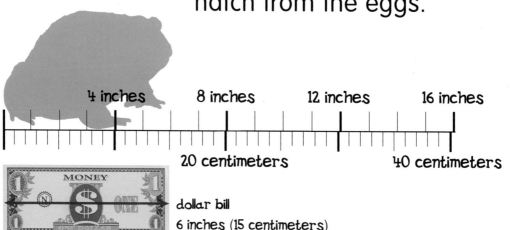

4 inches   8 inches   12 inches   16 inches

20 centimeters   40 centimeters

dollar bill
6 inches (15 centimeters)

Glands behind the toads' eyes produce a **poison**
The poison stops **predators** from eating the toads.

Fire Salamander

Fire **salamanders** live in forests in Africa, Europe, and western Asia. They eat worms, slugs, and bugs.

Their yellow and black marks warn predators that salamanders have poison on their skin. Fire salamanders can also spray their poison at predators.

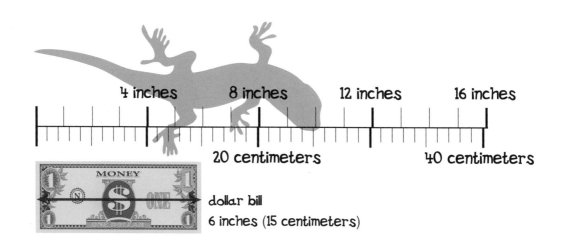

4 inches   8 inches   12 inches   16 inches

20 centimeters   40 centimeters

dollar bill
6 inches (15 centimeters)

Baby fire salamanders are called **larvae**. They live in ponds and streams and can breathe underwater just like fish.

When they grow up, they live on land and breathe air like humans. They are one of the largest kinds of salamanders.

Great Crested Newt

Great crested newts live near ponds and lakes in Europe. Adult newts spend the summer or entire year in water.

During the daytime, they hide under logs or stones. At night, they look for food. They eat tadpoles, worms, and bug larvae.

A male great crested newt has a jagged **crest**. The crest grows bigger during breeding season.

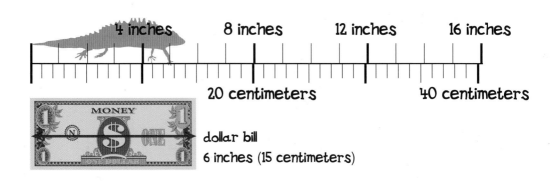

4 inches   8 inches   12 inches   16 inches

20 centimeters   40 centimeters

dollar bill
6 inches (15 centimeters)

Female newts lay two to three eggs
every day for about five months.
They wrap their eggs in leaves and
hide them among water plants.

female

Larvae hatch from the eggs
and live in the water until
they become adults. Then
they move onto the land.

Horned Frog

There are many types of horned frog. This large **species** lives in the rain forest in South America and Asia.

The Asian horned frog has a huge head. Two big bumps stick out above its eyes. They look like horns and keep predators away.

Females can lay up to one thousand eggs. They wrap them around plants in the water.

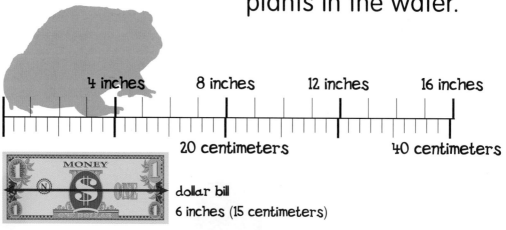

4 inches   8 inches   12 inches   16 inches

20 centimeters   40 centimeters

dollar bill
6 inches (15 centimeters)

Horned frogs bury themselves in the ground when they hunt their prey. They pounce on passing lizards, mice, and other frogs.

This Chacoan horned frog lives in South America. It will eat almost anything that moves!

Japanese Giant Salamander

Japanese giant salamanders are the biggest amphibians in the world. They live in cold mountain streams and rivers in Japan.

Japanese giant salamanders eat many different animals, including crabs, bugs, mice, and fish. They can go for weeks without eating if there is no food.

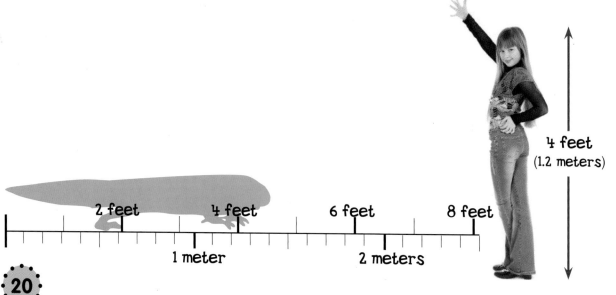

4 feet
(1.2 meters)

2 feet   4 feet   6 feet   8 feet

1 meter   2 meters

Females lay about five hundred eggs in long strings in holes dug by males. Males guard the eggs until they hatch. They become very fierce if predators come near the eggs.

Japanese giant salamanders breathe through their skin. **Organs** along their bodies help them **detect** their prey.

Mud Puppy

Mud puppies are a type of salamander. They live in freshwater in southern Canada and in the central and eastern United States.

Female mud puppies dig a nest under rocks and logs to lay their eggs. They guard their eggs until they hatch, about two months later.

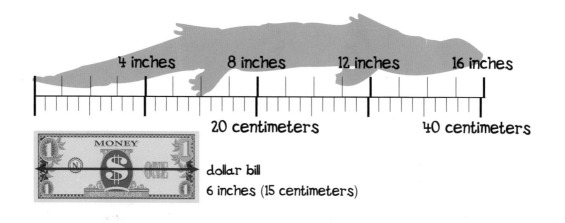

4 inches   8 inches   12 inches   16 inches

20 centimeters   40 centimeters

dollar bill
6 inches (15 centimeters)

Mud puppies are brown, grey, or black.
Blue-black spots cover their bodies.

Feathery gills grow from their heads.
The dark red gills remove **oxygen** from
the water.

North American Bullfrog

North American bullfrogs eat other frogs, **reptiles**, birds, fish, and fish eggs. They will even eat other bullfrogs!

Bullfrogs live in lakes, ponds, and streams. They like shallow, warm water.

They can leap 6 feet (2 meters) with their long, strong back legs. People sometimes eat bullfrog legs.

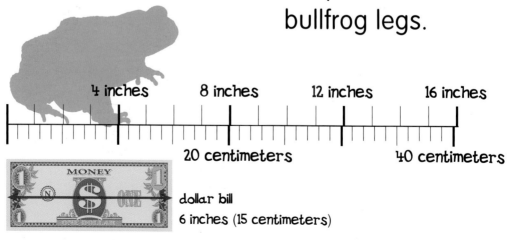

4 inches   8 inches   12 inches   16 inches

20 centimeters   40 centimeters

dollar bill
6 inches (15 centimeters)

The round circles behind the eyes are the frog's ears. Males have larger ears than females.

Male bullfrogs protect their **territory** from other frogs. They warn other frogs with loud noises, wrestle with them, or chase them off.

Poison Dart Frog

Poison dart frogs live in rain forests in Central America. People use the frogs' poison on their arrows and darts to kill their prey.

Female green poison dart frogs lay five to thirteen eggs beneath a leaf or log. When the eggs hatch, the male or female frogs carry the tadpoles on their backs to a stream, pond, or tree hole filled with water.

Poison dart frogs can be red, blue, or green.

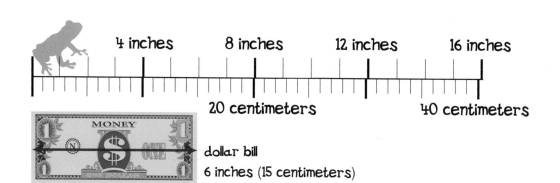

4 inches   8 inches   12 inches   16 inches

20 centimeters   40 centimeters

dollar bill
6 inches (15 centimeters)

Their bright colors help defend them from attack. They warn predators that the frog is **poisonous.**

Tree Frog

Tree frogs live in Australia, New Guinea, Europe, Asia, and North and South America. There are more than seven hundred species of tree frogs.

Tree frogs have sticky pads on their fingers and toes to help them climb trees. These frogs usually come out at night looking for bugs to eat.

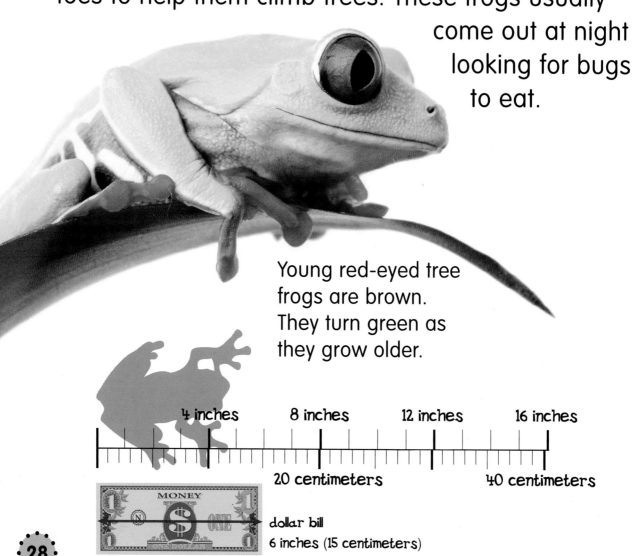

Young red-eyed tree frogs are brown. They turn green as they grow older.

4 inches 8 inches 12 inches 16 inches

20 centimeters 40 centimeters

dollar bill
6 inches (15 centimeters)

Giant tree frogs are the largest type of tree frog. They can grow to nearly 5 inches (12 centimeters).

Female tree frogs lay their eggs in water. The White's tree frog can lay up to three thousand eggs at one time!

For More Information

Books to Read

Bishop, Nic. *Frogs*. Scholastic Nonfiction

Curtis, Jennifer Keats. *Turtles in My Sandbox*. Sylvan Dell Publishing

Kalman, Bobbie. *Frogs and Other Amphibians*. Crabtree Publishing Company

Kolpin, Molly. *Newts*. Pebble Plus

Moffet, Mark. *Face to Face with Frogs*. National Geographic

Ryder, Joanne. *Toad by the Road: A Year in the Life of These Amazing Amphibians*. Henry Holt and Company, LLC

Places to Explore

Aquarium of the Pacific
100 Aquarium Way
Long Beach, CA 90802
www.aquariumofpacific.org
Learn about the California coastal range newt, the golden poison dart frog, and the cane toad, as well as other amphibians.

National Zoo
3001 Connecticut Avenue NW,
Washington, DC 20008
nationalzoo.si.edu
Check out the Reptile Discovery Center and Amazonia building of this free zoo.

Reptile and Amphibian Discovery Zoo
3297 County Road 45 N,
Owatonna, MN 55060-6228
www.theradzoo.com
Pet amphibians at this zookeeper-run, family-owned zoo in southeastern Minnesota.

Shedd Aquarium
1200 South Lake Shore Drive
Chicago, IL 60605
www.sheddaquarium.org
Plan to spend the day at this state-of-the-art aquarium, where amphibians thrive among thirty-two thousand aquatic animals.

Web Sites to Visit

animals.nationalgeographic.com/animals/amphibians/warty-newt
Meet the warty newt and watch videos of other amphibians.

ethemes.missouri.edu/themes/782?locale=zh
Dip into this list of websites about amphibians, where you'll find everything from an interactive chart of an amphibian's body to videos, games, and clip art.

www.learninggamesforkids.com/animal-games-amphibians.html
Hunt for the blue spotted salamander and poison dart frogs in two videos among others about amphibians.

www.sandiegozoo.org/animalbytes/t-salamander.html
Find out about newts and salamanders and more from this zoo site.

Publisher's note: We have reviewed these Web sites to ensure that they are suitable for children. Web sites change frequently, however, so children should be closely supervised whenever they access the Internet.

Glossary

breed — to make baby animals

continents — huge sheets of rock floating on Earth's surface. The seven large land areas on Earth are continents.

crest — a growth on an animal's body

detect — to discover or find out information

gills — parts of an animal used for taking in oxygen under water

glands — parts of the body that make special chemicals needed for the body to work well

hatch — to break out of an egg

larvae — the young that hatch out of the eggs of many insects, other bugs, and other animals. Larvae often look like small worms. As they get older, they change into their adult form.

organs — parts of the body, such as the heart, lungs, or stomach, that do specific jobs

oxygen — a gas that has no smell or color. People, animals, and plants need oxygen to live. Animals that live on land usually breathe in oxygen with their lungs. Animals that live in the water usually get oxygen using their gills.

poison — substance that can kill or hurt an animal or person

poisonous — causing sickness or death by poison

predators — animals that hunt other animals for food

prey — animals that are hunted for food

reptiles — animals that are cold-blooded and have scaly skin. Reptiles breathe air. Most reptiles lay eggs, but some give birth to live babies.

salamanders — animals that are usually covered with smooth, moist skin and often look like lizards. Salamanders do not have scales.

scientists — people who use science to find out information about the world

slugs — animals that look like snails without shells. Some slugs have tiny shells.

species — a group of living things of the same type

tadpoles — the young form of frogs and toads. Tadpoles have round bodies and long tails. They live in water and breathe with gills.

territory — the area where an animal lives. Animals guard their territories to stop other animals from eating the food in that area.

Index